T0273757

Matty May

If You Love Me
This Might Hurt

Salamander Street

PLAYS

First published in 2021 by Salamander Street Ltd.
(info@salamanderstreet.com)

If You Love Me This Might Hurt © Matty May, 2021

All rights reserved.

Application for professional and amateur performance rights should be directed to the author c/o Salamander Street. No performance may be given unless a licence has been obtained, and no alterations may be made in the title or the text of the adaptation without the author's prior written consent.

You may not copy, store, distribute, transmit, reproduce or otherwise make available this publication (or any part of it) in any form, or binding or by any means (print, electronic, digital, optical, mechanical, photocopying, recording or otherwise), without the prior written permission of the publisher. Any person who does any unauthorized act in relation to this publication may be liable to criminal prosecution and civil claims for damages.

ISBN: 9781914228513

10 9 8 7 6 5 4 3 2 1

Care has been at the forefront of making this work. Without the care of so many wonderful people I would not have been able to write the words you're about to read. Care has been in place for everyone who has been a part of this creative process and we have all done our best to look after each other. This care should be felt by audiences when the work is performed. We hold each other in this space as we do in this life, it's how we get through.

If You Love Me This Might Hurt was first performed at Camden People's Theatre on 19 October 2021.

The creative team was as follows:

Writer and performer **Matty May**

Director **Scott Le Crass**

Producer **Daisy Hale**

Designer **Katherina Radeva**

Sound Designer **Annie May Fletcher**

Lighting Designer **Lauren Woodhead**

Dramaturgy **Scott Le Crass and Scottee**

Technical Stage Manager **Amy Daniels**

Assistant Producer **Sean Brooks**

Image by **Corinne Cumming**

Design by **Dani Vazquez**

'Hello' by Adele plays. ~ This text is performed over the track with lip-syncing between lines.

Oh, don't mind me. Are we all settled in okay? Has everyone got a bev? Great.

(Lip-sync.)

In this show I talk about suicide a lot and I do also talk about hurting myself. I think it's important that you know that I feel able to do this, it feels safe for me to talk about this.

(Lip-sync.)

Let's make an agreement that if you want to leave the room for a bit then you're allowed to do that and you're welcome to come back in, okay? This ain't like normal theatre. Although don't take the piss and be in and out every five minutes alright.

(Lip-sync.)

Now, are we all ready?

Let's begin.

(Adele fades out.)

When you're like me you're not allowed to be angry. That's not the part you're meant to play. You're the nice boy, the sensitive boy and as you get older, you're the funny boy. The camp boy. So, what ya do is, you take that anger and you bury it. You push it right down into the pit of your stomach.

You're scared of people seeing that ugly, ugly rage. You don't know how to say that there's a sadness in you that makes everything hurt.

So, you do your best to hide it with eyeliner, bright clothes and loud laughs. But it's there, you can't keep burying it so eventually it comes out.

There's only so much you can hold in that pit of your stomach and so of course it's going to come out…

So you drink. Because that's what people do. And it's fun. You're drinking, dancing, laughing, I mean fuck you're an inspirational quote and babe you don't care who's watching.

And then something shifts.

That buried rage sees an opportunity. It tricks you. This is fun, don't stop now.

Keep going.

Another one.

And something switches.

You're not laughing anymore.

You're argumentative. You're ready for a fight. You don't know how to tell them that this overwhelming sadness is unbearable and you don't know how to say I think I'd be better off... so you act like a cunt.

You become aggressive just like the men you hate.

This isn't the real me. This is the me I don't like. This is the me with the spiteful tongue.

And you're always sorry. You wake up and you know instantly. Even if you can't remember what actually happened you feel it in the pit of your stomach.

The shame.

The sweat.

Your whole body feels like it's drowning.

You apologise.

You promise it will never happen again. *(Longer pause.)* You can't let it go though. You mull it over for months and it joins your long list of mistakes.

You're the one you hurt the most.

Beginning

Is it annoying to have a bit called the beginning ten minutes in?

My name is Matty May. I was born on the 29th of April 1989 on what my Nan Jan will swear to you was the sunniest Saturday Barking has ever seen.

When she talks about that day which she always does at least once a year on my birthday, the look on her face makes it impossible to believe that the sun doesn't shine out of my arse. She doesn't see the messiness, the complexity, she sees that special little boy. That sunny Saturday.

When I talk about my Nan, I don't think she's what most people would imagine when they hear that word. She's not a little old lady with a tight perm who smells like custard creams. She was only thirty-nine when I was born. She's got a filthy laugh, makes blowjob jokes, has a really posh telephone voice and is a terrible flirt. She's gentle, and carries a lot on her shoulders. She's quite something.

(Longer pause.)

I was conceived in July 1988 on that same Nan Jan's sofa, in Nan Jan's pink house. It's pink because my Nan couldn't decide on a colour, so my Grandad did it one day while she was at work. That house felt like the safest place in the world. It felt consistent. A place where you weren't second guessing yourself or trying to anticipate what might happen next. I spent a lot of time doing that, so the pink house was a respite.

At my Nan's I'd have dippy eggs, soldiers and a cup of milk for my breakfast, all from matching crockery which had my name on it. I'd play with my matching pink iron and ironing board. I'd watch *The Bodyguard* and *Three Men and a Baby* over and over again. Like literally finish watching it, rewind it and start it again. Consistent.

The bedroom where I slept was called Nanny's make-up room, at least I've always known it as that. A treasure trove of costume jewellery, pretty dresses, huge shoulder pads, high heeled shoes, and of course as the name suggests, make-up. Using the huge fluffy brush that tickled a bit to put on the blusher and adding lashings of lipstick. At bed time in this room we'd read stories and sing goodnight sweetheart like the men in *Three Men and a Baby*.

Sorry, I've digressed.

I was conceived in July 1988 on my Nan Jan's sofa. I came from a one-night stand between my Mum and a bloke called Bobby, who was her brother's best mate. It was fuelled by alcohol and possibly lust, but mainly a cock full of Stella. I don't think there was love, although maybe it was said in the heat of the moment.

Mark

My Mum met Mark, the man who raised me, when I was three and married him when I was four. Before they met it had always just been us.

My Mum was mine.

I remember screaming from the back seat of his car because my Mum had sat next to him in the front. I remember crying and screaming and I imagine I must have seemed like a right little brat trying to get his own way. Actually, I was scared. I'd seen my Mum hurt before. I'd heard the shouting and seen the blood and I just wanted to protect her. I wanted us to stay as just us two because by three I already knew that men were dangerous.

(Longer pause.)

Mark scared me. I could tell that I annoyed him, even when I tried really hard not to.

One day we're in the car on the way to Southend. I was sitting in the front passenger seat because I used to get car sick.

It was sunny and 'Life' by Des'ree came on. It's one of those songs that is so bad that it's actually quite wonderful and so I'm singing. He smacks me across the back of the head and says, "I told you to shut the fuck up" and turned the radio off.

I think cars were invented to give us all somewhere to sing. Cars without music don't make sense to me.

I don't think Mark thought he was too strict, too violent, too much. His own Dad had used a belt on him regularly, so in his mind, anything less than that was fair game.

I assumed he'd kick me out once he knew I was gay. I was gonna go and live in the pink house with my Nan. I'd planned it.

He didn't kick me out though. When my Mum sent him upstairs to my room to talk about it he sat on my bed and cried. I sat on the swivel chair in my room facing away from him. He didn't cry because he was angry or disappointed but because he loved me.

He said, "I don't care that you're... ya know." and then he said he loved me. He loved me. Imagine that right, you've spent your whole life trying to understand why this man hates you so much. Why everything you do annoys him, what sort of little boy you could be to make him like you, and just when you get to the point in the story that you've prepared for, the bit when he calls you a queer, kicks the shit out of you and throws you onto the street, all he can do is cry and tell you he loves you.

Crying in front of me in fact for only the third time, the first being when he was telling me that my Mum had cheated, and the second being when his own Dad had died.

So, I understand what love can look like when you're a bit fucked up.

(Question to the audience.) Are we all doing alright? Great.

Bobby

Then there's Bobby. The biological Dad. The one-night stand on Nan Jan's sofa. A one-night stand but also my uncle's best mate, so when I was twenty and wanted to meet him I just went to my uncle's Facebook friends list and typed in 'Bobby'.

He was only nineteen when he got my Mum pregnant and from what I can gather he wasn't ready, or didn't want to be ready or something like that.

To be fair to him he didn't actually know that he was my Dad until the day of my first birthday, which my Mum combined with a Christening and had two gorgeous blue and white cakes made. I don't know how that conversation happened, but I imagine alcohol might have been involved.

There's a photo of him holding me at that birthday but I don't know if he's holding me thinking I'm his best mate's nephew, or if he's holding me after he's been told I'm his son.

(Longer pause.)

When I was a kid I hated him a lot of the time because I didn't understand what I'd done wrong. Sometimes when I was walking to school I used to imagine that he was gonna drive up to me and hand me a bag of money. He'd robbed a bank and had to leave because he was on the run, but he wanted me to have this money because he loved me and because he was sorry.

We accidentally met each other once. I'm twelve, I'm staying at my Nan and Grandad's for the weekend and we go to the Harrow pub.

He's there. He calls me Matthew which feels formal and he asks me how school is.

What I want to say is that it's none of your business you useless cunt. *(Longer pause.)*

What I say instead is something along the lines of *(Mumbles.)* "Yeah it's fine thanks." *(Pause.)*

A few months after I found him on Facebook I went to his birthday party. We ended up back at his place with some of his mates and got a couple of grams in. We all talked shit and snorted lines off the kitchen counter until the early hours, as you do with your Dad.

Dave

There's a version of this show where Dave isn't mentioned at all.

His importance has faded in recent years and I'm thankful for that. So all I'll say is this. For a time Dave was a disruption in the flat where me and my Mum lived. One day when the three of us were in that flat a man jumped from a window in the tower block opposite. I don't know why.

I have a recurring dream where me and my Mum are trying to escape from Dave. My Mum has thrown the house phone out of the flat window and we both frantically try to climb down the telephone wire before he catches us. Escaping from the window just like the man in the block opposite.

That's enough.

I had a therapist who I paid £50 a week for about eighteen months. She suggested that perhaps the reason I seemed to be more interested in the men that treated me badly or that messed me around was because there was a desire in me to prove that I could make men love me. That I could earn their love.

Telly

I knew I was weird before I knew what weird meant, and by weird I mean well, you know what I mean. I didn't know exactly what it was that made me weird, I just knew that it scared me. I started to understand my weirdness through moments I saw on the telly. Like the day I wasn't well so had the day off school, *The Vanessa Feltz Show* was on and there was a guest on the show who was effeminate. Everyone on the stage talking to him seemed very upset and they kept using this word gay. I didn't know what that word meant, but I instinctively knew that I was like this person.

I can't explain the confusion, excitement and fear I felt the night I saw Tony and Simon kiss for the first time on *EastEnders*. Although Tiffany was my favourite character and I understood that her brother and boyfriend kissing wasn't completely right, it did mean that things started to make sense a little.

Sneaking out of bed, turning the old telly that I had in my bedroom on to watch snippets of *Queer as Folk* with the sound on one.

My Mum, clutching her lottery tickets tight in her hand waiting to see if we were rich, and me being terrified of the person pressing the button that night. He was wearing a big green hat and make-up, but I was sure this person was a man. I thought about it all the time, that I was like his person. A few days later I sat in the bath crying my eyes out because I was scared of being weird. My Mum came running in, helped me out of the bath, wrapped a towel around me and asked me repeatedly what was wrong. I was crying too much to talk, but even when i could I instinctively knew this was something I shouldn't talk about.

Fat Queer

At fifteen I started going to Slimming World and I lost weight really quickly. Every week I'd go to the meetings and the group leader would get me to explain how I'd done so well. I'd say I managed to stick to the diet because I know I'll be happier when I'm thin, which makes lots of the fat women at the meeting cry.

At this point I've got a group of mates where it feels like I can pretty much be myself. We're a mix of boys and girls, I'm the funny one so it's alright that I'm a bit different to the other boys. and we all hang out together in Tubbies. Tubbies is a bit of green near the train station and it's called that because it has four big hills like the ones in the *Teletubbies* opening credits. The hills are really useful because you can see if the police show up. You have time to warn everyone to stash their drink and run.

I've been trying really hard to be normal, I even asked for the *Hollyoaks* Babe's calendar at Christmas and tried my best to look at it while I wanked. One of the boys has made it really hard to ignore that I'm… ya know.

He's called Rob. He's a bit immature but he really makes me laugh. We hang about together loads and still manage to have stuff to say when we talk on the phone and MSN Messenger. A couple of times we hold hands. One time we nearly kissed. Sometimes when I stay at his house, he flashes his willy and laughs.

After a while our friendship starts to change though. The initial fun and laughter is still there sometimes, but other times it turns into massive arguments. It's really intense, almost like we're going out with each other. We're not though.

(Pause.)

Sarah's sixteenth birthday. Her Mum has stayed at her mates for the night so we can have her flat.

A free house. This means we have somewhere to get pissed. Free houses are Lambrini and greasy chicken shop boxes. They're where first fingerings happen, they smell like Joop aftershave and sound like 00's R&B and Garage.

(Pause.)

There's a tension between me and Rob. I've spent most of the night avoiding him which I know winds him up – I haven't been subtle about it either. I can't bear to be around him but am also desperate for his attention. We're both standing in the kitchen and an argument starts. He pushes me and I fall against the counter. I grab hold of him and someone throws the first attempt at a drunken punch. Neither one of us is much of a fighter but there's a lot of rage and we end up having to be pulled apart in the kitchen. People are standing between us. We're shouting and I get dragged out to the hallway.

I walk into the bathroom, grab my friend's Mum's razor and cut my arms.

Not particularly deep. More like a frantic scratch that tears the skin. This is what I've been doing some times.

I pull the sleeves of my hoody down and go into one of the bedrooms. Someone finds blood in the bathroom and works out it's me. Next thing, some of the girls are crying and I'm barricaded in the kitchen with two of them blocking the door so no one else can come in. One of my friends says it's really fucking weird to do that, but she doesn't mean it horribly, I think she's just scared.

Rob bangs on the door repeatedly until someone lets him in.

He holds my hands and tries not to cry. I love you Matt, he says to me. I can't look at him. I'm standing there with blood on my arms in the tiny kitchen of this council flat and around us is commotion, other drunk teenagers, but I feel like it's just us.

I want so much for him to mean that he loves me in the way that I love him because he's all I think about, and no matter how hard I try to push him out of my thoughts I just can't and I end up cumming or crying.

You're like my brother, he says.

But I don't want to be his brother.

Well actually I wouldn't mind being his actual brother coz he's proper fit and I imagine he could pull anyone he wants. Sometimes when I'm round their house he comes into the room they share in just a towel or his Calvin Klein's and I try to snapshot that moment in my memory.

I want Rob to never let go of my hands. I'm convinced that if he holds them really tight he might be able to fix me.

That night changes everything. This not-very-sweet sixteen happens right at the end of August, just before we start sixth form. The friends I had aren't the friends I have anymore. I have the girls and Rob has the boys. Rooms go silent when I walk through the door apart from whispers and laughter. A lot of people don't say hello.

(Pause.)

The girls have become more than friends. They're my protectors. Don't fuck about with working-class women, their instinct to protect is second to none. Like this one day in school, one of the girls is desperately trying to stop me from going into the sixth form block but refusing to tell me why. When I do eventually go in there I see another one of the girls screaming at one of the boys about what a prick he is as she pulls pieces of paper off of the wall. Some of the boys have made posters with my face on, and in big bold font, the words 'fat queer'.

(Question to the audience.) Are we all doing okay? Just a reminder that we agreed earlier you can take a minute if you need to.

Mum

There was a time when just me and my Mum lived in our council flat. The flat had brown carpet and she had big curly hair and gold earrings. My Mum would get out the shake and vac, I would sprinkle while she would follow behind me with the hoover, and Whitney would give us the soundtrack.

My Mum has a pain in her wrist. Every now and then when you're with her she'll hold it and twist her hand.

She never talks about why and I don't know if she remembers. My Mum and Dad had been out.

I can't think of many times this happened that didn't end in a screaming row. Inevitably they arrived home separately and she screamed repeatedly up the stairs. I go to bed while they shout at each other in the bedroom next door.

My sister is a baby and she cries.

Inevitably my Mum comes into my room.

She lays herself down on the bottom bunk of my dark green metal bunk beds.

Argumentative.

This is not my real Mum.

This is the Mum I don't like.

This is the Mum with the spiteful tongue.

I don't remember the build-up but obviously I'm not pitying her. I'm not agreeing with her. All I want is for her to be quiet because I know my Dad can hear every word and I know he might burst into the room like he has before.

She begins to taunt me and eventually she says what always comes out when she's in this pissed-up state.

"You should be on my side," she begins.

"He's not your real Dad. He doesn't love you like I do. I'm your Mum, nobody loves you the way I do."

This goes on. I ask her so many times to be quiet.

The rage is building up inside me and instead of asking her to be quiet I tell her to shut up. She doesn't. She has that glazed look in her eye and all I want is for her to stop and I'm begging her to please just go to sleep but she won't.

I'm stood on the green metal ladder halfway between the top and bottom bunk.

I see her wrist is hanging over the metal bar at the end of the bed and as she laughs that spiteful fake laugh I lower my foot and with full force stamp on her wrist repeatedly.

Rage.

She lets out a sound and begins to cry immediately. I jump up onto my top bunk and I lay there silently.

"How could you do that to your Mum?" she says.

I don't answer because I don't know.

My throat is full of some kind of phlegmy liquid that I want to spit out but I don't make a sound.

I lay silently, my eyes squeezed tight. I know that I am not a nice boy or a lovely boy anymore.

I am just like them.

I am just like the men who rage at my Mum. The ones who have no control and make her cry.

I lay there thinking that she made me do it, so I even think with the same excuse those men do.

(Pause.)

We're all so much more than one thing aren't we.

My Mum is the sort of person who would give you her last fiver if you needed it. She desperately wants to make everyone around her happy, and she bears the weight of that. She is a carer too, just like my Nan.

She's a worrier. She worries all the time. She worries about me. I'm a worrier too, and I worry about her, so I think we both spend a lot of time worrying about each other.

She tried making a cake out of a packet once and ended up baking the icing instead of the cake mix. She finds her own farts really funny and so do I.

Maybe I'm over explaining, spoon feeding you to make absolutely sure that you remember that no person is just one thing, because we're all complex and complicated to different extents.

It's just that I don't think we always allow that complexity, that messiness to take the space that it deserves.

We're understanding of mental health problems when they present themselves in a way that is palatable to us.

If your version of unwell looks like needing some time under your duvet and a day or two off work we get that. Or if you're able to communicate your distress in a long form Instagram post then we feel comfortable commenting that we're there for you.

But when it's the darker uglier stuff, that's when we get wary. If your coping mechanism is drinking yourself into oblivion and causing a scene, that might make us all a bit uncomfortable.

One

It's 2007. I'm eighteen and I set off for uni. I was sure this would be a new beginning. A second chance.

I'd pinned every hope of happiness on… Portsmouth and the people I was gonna meet there. I had it all planned out.

I had my wardrobe of slogan T-shirts, every colour of fingerless gloves imaginable, dyed jet-black hair and enough eyeliner to fuel a 2005 Myspace convention.

I was ready to find my people.

I was ready to dive in head-first and be friended and fucked and loved and appreciated by my fellow gays.

The first few weeks were a blur of nights out, £2 double vodkas and jugs of snakebite.

I didn't eat much for the first few weeks. I tried to stick to tins of Heinz soup with a little bit of pasta added in.

I don't meet any gay people though.

I go to the LGBT society once. I feel like people look me up and down with judgemental eyes. It wasn't what I expected. it hurts because I was hoping to feel safe here, but I don't, I feel uncomfortable. I feel odd and awkward. I don't think it's their fault, it's me. I just don't fit here either.

I don't go back. I go to the clubs where my straight friends go. Sometimes I'm the entertainment and other times I'm the liability. Sometimes I feel unsafe around the groups of straight men. Occasionally there's comments but amongst that there are a few who really like me. They find me funny. With some of them it's more than that. There's an intense curiosity.

(Pause.)

The first time I tried to kill myself was frantic. I was drunk. It wasn't pre-planned in any definite sense, but it was something I'd thought about most days for as long as I could remember. It didn't happen because I was drunk, but alcohol was like a lubricant, it helped me push past the other voice.

It's a student house so there's alcohol and plenty of paracetamol for the morning after.

I started to swallow. The Paracetamol were the cheap ones that weren't coated, the sort that start to fall apart as soon as they touch your mouth making them hard to swallow when taken in large quantities. *(Pause.)*

I cut myself with a razorblade.

I'm not telling you how to try and pornify it or glamourise it or any of that stuff. But it's what happened, and I think that maybe if I name it you won't spend the rest of the show trying to work out what method I tried.

I remember the ambulance person seeming a bit impatient. Actually, that's not true. I know from my own moments lapsing in and out of consciousness and from what my friend told me that they weren't just impatient. They were dismissive and belittling.

Time waster. That's what people call it, don't they? I wonder at what point you stop being a time waster. Do you have to be dead? Are you a time waster unless you die? Are those the two options?

Time waster, or, shit too late, they're dead. Then it's sad. That's so sad, isn't it? Isn't that sad. You're a time waster until you're dead.

When I woke up in hospital my stomach was cramping and before I can even open my eyes, I was sick. "That will be all the tablets you took my darling," a nice nurse said as she wiped me.

I realised I was surrounded by old people. I was on a geriatric ward because that's where there was space. I felt guilty because all these people were desperately trying to stay alive, and these nurses and doctors were wasting time on me. Shame.

(Pause.)

I felt so lonely. The only number the hospital had was my next of kin. My Mum. I told them in no circumstances were they to call my Mum.

I needed a wee for hours, but I was hooked up to lots of drips and machines and I didn't want to be any more of a pain than I already had been so I didn't say anything.

When my friends came to see me, I cried because I thought they were just going to leave me there.

I kept my head turned to the side.

One held my hand. One couldn't look at me. One asked me why. Why? Now that's what really hurts isn't it. I can't tell you why, I've already upset you enough.

I said sorry and I meant it. Sorry for hurting them and sorry I was still here.

(Pause.)

The nice nurse who had short cropped hair and looked a bit like my mate Bradley's aunty Lorraine was the one who took my cannula out. Then she said to me,

"If I had a son as lovely as you, I'd really want to know if he'd been in the hospital. I'd hate to think he might be going through this and didn't think he could tell me."

I knew she meant well by saying this to me, but she didn't know that my Mum was a bit broken too.

The hospital gave me a number to call to set up some counselling.

After the assessment they tell me they have a space on Monday nights at 8 o'clock. I never went back. Monday night was my favourite night out at uni.

Two

Sometimes we need to be able to laugh at these things.

After I finished uni, I worked in an office to save up and go travelling to South East Asia, which my family thought was quite fancy.

When I get home from travelling, I'm tanned and I'm the skinniest I've ever been. Everyone keeps telling me how amazing I look and I thrive on that. The thing is though being this much smaller hasn't fixed everything the way I thought it would. Just like going to uni didn't fix it, or travelling didn't fix it.

I knew I was going to do it this time. I thought about it constantly.

I thought about hanging myself a lot, but I thought I'd probably end up doing it wrong… I'm not very good at practical stuff like that.

I didn't want my Mum to find me, so I went to Tubbies. I fail again. What am I like?

I didn't give the hospital permission to call my Mum, but she'd called the police because she was worried about me. I told you she was always worrying.

I am looking at the door to the ward when my Mum walks in.

Her face is in a state I know too well. She's been crying. She catches my eye from across the ward and tries to give me a smile. Worry is etched across her face.

When she's next to me she squeezes my hand tight, like her grip alone might be the thing to fix me.

Even through the worry she seems so strong in a way I've never felt before. Like it's her life's mission to protect me.

When the Doctor comes over, he says that he can see on my notes that this is the second time this has happened.

"No it's not!" my Mum says.

(Pause.)

"You must have the wrong notes," she says.

They both look at me.

"It's not, is it boy?"

I stay silent. Tears start to roll slowly down my face.

When the Doctor leaves she holds my hand even tighter than before and kisses it for the longest time.

She wipes the tears from my cheeks and leans into me and says, "Why didn't you tell Mummy."

In that moment I realise that I've snatched away from her the one thing she considers herself to be good at. She sees me as the thing she got right, and now she feels like she has failed, twice.

My Mum tells me later that they considered sectioning me and I know that I'm meant to be relieved that they didn't, but actually I wished that they had. Not out loud, but in my head.

When I'm allowed home, I sleep a lot. I wake up late one morning and can hear that soothing voice. It's my Nan, she's calling my Mum darling in that gentle way that I recognise from times when I've been upset. I can tell they are cuddling from the way their voices sound. My Mum is properly crying but trying to do it as quietly as possible. It's like she's tried really hard to be strong for me and now she can let it all out because her own Mum's here.

My Nan comes into my room and leans down next to my bed. She strokes her hand across my face and calls me darling. She talks to me in her gentle voice. I don't know what to say. She tells me that she loves me so much and that she can't imagine this world without me. She wraps her arms around me and we cry together. I know that to her I am still that sunny Saturday morning.

The following days are full of conversations with people who don't know what to say. They're trying not to cry and asking me why I did it. Why?

Annie Lennox 'Why' plays (lip-sync).

Platform

I'm in this straight club for my mate's birthday. The music is okay. The drinks are expensive. It feels like the sort of place you might go if you go out in London once a year with the lads. Me and my mate lose the others and she goes to the toilet. I stand waiting on the edge of a light-up dance floor. This is one of those clubs with seventy-five different rooms and so not many people are really dancing on this one. It's just where you stand while your mates are at the bar or having a piss. While I'm standing there a man walks up to me. The music is loud and he says something I don't hear. I say I can't hear you when I probably should've just walked away and then he says something else that ends with the word faggot. When I open my eyes I'm laying on the light up dance floor and blood is pouring out of my mouth. The music has stopped. The room emptied. It feels like someone has ripped the left side of my mouth open and all I can taste is the sticky thickness of blood.

I get taken to the hospital. A nurse stitches my lip back together and the policeman has to leave me. I still don't know where my friends are. I wonder if they think it was my fault because of the times I've been drunk before and acted like a twat. I want to explain to them that I honestly didn't do anything wrong. That I can remember the entire night. That I didn't start anything or try it on with him or any of the things they might be thinking. I wonder if they're sick of me.

I ask the nurse if there is any way she or someone else might have a phone charger I could borrow. She says they don't. They X-ray my neck and my jaw. They give me strong pain killers and let me sleep for a bit. The nurse wakes me up she tells me that the X-ray is fine and I'm free to go.

I wonder if they might offer me some sort of lift. They don't. I feel guilty for expecting a lift because I know that's a waste of money, but I just feel a bit scared. They discharge me with a packet of Co-codamol and point me in the direction of the tube station.

It's early on a Sunday morning, the trains haven't long started running. People stare at my swollen stitched-up mouth and the blood that's all over my shirt. The platform is quiet and I stand right on the edge. I wonder if anyone in the hospital looked at my notes before they sent me off with my packets of strong painkillers. I wonder if they thought about the fact I was on my own after just being attacked and the fact I didn't have a phone. I stand on the yellow lines and I think about how my face, my voice provokes such rage. Shall I jump? Shall I jump? Should I be brave and jump. Would it be the rest I want?

The train is now approaching please stand back from the platform edge. This isn't the first time I've thought about this or stood on the edge of a platform. The train is now approaching, please stand back from the platform edge. An empty platform at a station in central London must be quite a rarity. The train is now approaching, she announces again, like she's talking directly to me.

On the train I look at the floor. A woman sitting opposite me asks if I'm okay. I got punched, I say.

(Question to the audience.) How are we all doing? Okay, let's continue.

Three

I've recently been made redundant, but luckily I've found a new job almost straight away.

I'm living in a flat share that has a balcony that looks out over London and it's beautiful.

I feel like the loneliest person in the world.

I find myself with weekends with no plans. I'm embarrassed by my loneliness, so I lie.

When my flatmates get home I pretend to have arrived not long before them. I binge on takeaways and chocolate and crisps and I have an internal dialogue where I justify the calories to myself because I'm not out drinking.

Then I go back down to the shop underneath my flat and I buy a bottle or two of cheap white wine.

I convince myself that I like to stay in even though I know that's a lie. I lay on the sofa thinking about how pathetic I am.

I open those apps on my phone and hope that someone will come and stop me feeling lonely for a little bit. I'm disgusted by my body.

I send messages of 'Hey, Hello and Hi'.

Even though the thought of bareback sex scares me I message people with names like 'BB only'. I say I'm not into chems when I get asked, then later I change my mind because it might be better than this silence.

A couple of times I get myself ready and walk the short distance to the Royal Vauxhall Tavern.

I stand across the road smoking. I try to build up the courage to go in. I don't. The thing is that by this point, I've been hurt too many times by my community. There's been one too many looks of judgement, nasty remarks and by this point I just assume there aren't spaces where I'll feel welcome.

A couple of times I end up at a sauna. I'm not about criticising those spaces, but what I needed was kindness. Putting myself, my body, this body in that space when I was already so vulnerable was self-harm.

I don't think there's anything more lonely than being penetrated by someone you're not attracted to, who you're pretty certain doesn't fancy you either.

I was completely sober this time. I started to feel the physical effects of what I've swallowed and even though I don't want to be alive the feeling of my body closing down scares me.

I walk up the stairs to the roof of our building.

I stand at the edge and I wonder if I'll find peace. I wonder how I'll feel as I fall through the air and if I'll feel it when I hit the ground.

I tell myself to do it. Just fucking do it.

I don't.

(Pause.)

This time at the hospital I decided that if there is even the smallest chance of things getting better, I have to be honest. When one of the mental health team asks me if I can guarantee my safety if they discharge me, I say no.

There's a pause.

She tells me that if I say no then they can't discharge me. I know, I say.

Another pause.

She tells me that the thing is, they don't have any beds, and anyway they only tend to keep people in for more mental health conditions.

She repeats the question, Matthew, can you guarantee your safety if I discharge you. I say yes.

I felt so ashamed. and I wonder if I should have been braver on the roof.

Why?

People think they want to know why but I'm not sure they do. You can't tell them the truth. If you do, if I do, I just feel like I'll be hurting them even more than I already have.

Why?

Because it feels inevitable. It feels impossible that this will end any other way. Like, no matter what I do, all paths lead to this.

Because of agonising loneliness. Not being able to shake the idea that you will end up that way.

Because I know I will destroy anything in my life that is good. That includes you, us. Eventually you will tire of me. I will find a way to ruin this.

Because life feels hard, and I am tired.

Because I worry all the time and I can't escape from that feeling of dread.

Because I don't think I've always been treated very nicely, and that mistreatment has shaped the way I treat myself.

Because of every person who has shouted faggot as I walk down the street. Because of the boys who plastered my face across the walls in school. Because of the – but not really. Not really because of those people.

Because of the ambulance person who was shit. Because I waited eighteen months for a therapy appointment after the third time I tried to die. But again, not really.

I don't know how much I can expect from you. I don't wanna spoon feed you, but I also don't want you to leave this space allowing yourself to over simplify this. Because it can't be reduced down like this can it?

Okay.

Because we live in a world of structures that make men think it's okay to attack, humiliate and destroy anyone that's different in order to prove their masculinity.

Because we have made a world that is unbearable and then we're surprised when people find it unbearable.

Because we exist in a world where we're shamed for needing help. It's a weakness.

Because care is something you must earn, and I don't know how to be worthy of it.

Because we're made to feel like we're failing, doing it wrong.

Because I can't imagine it getting any better.

Nan

After three, I went home to the pink house. You know there's always a place for you here, my nan said to me. Me and your Grandad both think it would be a pleasure to have you here.

In those first months, my Nan became my nurse. Unqualified, but trying her best to work out how to care for someone who has tried to kill themselves. Terrified of doing the wrong thing. Hiding every single object that could be a vehicle towards her worst nightmare. Trying to work out when to nudge, suggest something to eat or a shower. Knowing when to leave me in my room with my curtains closed.

When I say unqualified, I mean in the medical sense. In the sense that all you have is your gut instinct as someone who has always prioritised the care of others.

 She told me once, that when I walk through the front door with a huge smile on my face, that's when she worries most. She says that of course she loves to see me happy, but she's realised that this is when I'm most vulnerable. When things are going well, she says it's like I don't think I deserve it so I beat myself up and then inevitably I crash.

That must be exhausting. To be worrying about someone that much even when they seem happy. To be trying to anticipate what that person might need, where their head might go and what you might need to do to protect them from themselves.

My Nan will never watch this, but maybe one day I'll let her read this one bit, just in case it hasn't been clear enough when I write it in a birthday card, coz I'd hate to think she doesn't know.

I think you are wonderful. That you have anchored me amongst chaos.

I count myself so lucky to have you and I wonder what I'd be if I hadn't had you in my life.

I love that even in the absolute bleakest moments we can make each other laugh.

I worry about the day when you're not here anymore because I can't imagine the world without you.

And selfishly, I worry who will look after me the way you have looked after me? Because I always think about the people like me, who don't have someone like you to collapse entirely on to when things get messy and I don't know how they get by.

I think you are actually that sunny Saturday.

I'm saying all of this on the assumption that I'll be here longer than her, which doesn't always feel certain. I'll cut that last line out when I let her read this because it would only upset her. But it doesn't always feel that certain.

I think about four. I think about it because it feels like this world is becoming tougher, more rigid. That it's only getting harder to survive. It feels like there's less and less care, even less flexibility. Like it's purposely pushing some of us to find it unbearable.

I can't wrap this up for you. I can't end this with a promise that I'll be fine, that we'll be fine. It's messier than that – and I think I owe you that honesty.

The Spaniels 'Goodnight Sweetheart' plays' (lip-sync).

End.

Thank you to the entire creative team past and present for being a part of this and helping me make this happen through moments of self-doubt and fear.

To Dais for your encouragement, the pep talks and helping me see the possibilities.

To Scott for connecting with the work with softness and generosity.

Thank you to Scottee for showing me that fat common queers deserve space and for that first cup of tea that kickstarted all of this.

Also to Molly and Scottee & Friends who as a company have supported me and given me the opportunity to learn and grow.

To the team at Metal Peterborough who gave me a safe and generous space to start making this work.

To the team at Camden People's Theatre for supporting the show and me.

Thank you to Demi Nandhra for making *Life is No Laughing Matter* a piece of work that has stayed with me since I saw it.

Thank you to all of you that love me, my family and friends, my tripod and my gang. Your care, encouragement and love is valued more than you will ever know and the time we spend laughing together is when I am happiest.

Finally, thank you to Rico for bringing more joy to my life than I can ever explain.

This work is dedicated to my Nan Jan and to anyone who has found this world too hard to go on.

www.salamanderstreet.com

www.ingramcontent.com/pod-product-compliance
Lightning Source LLC
Jackson TN
JSHW011412130125
77033JS00024B/982